THE PRINCIPLES OF DEMOCRACY

WHAT IS
MAJORITY
RULE?

JOSHUA TURNER

PowerKiDS
press.

New York

Published in 2020 by The Rosen Publishing Group, Inc.
29 East 21st Street, New York, NY 10010

Copyright © 2020 by The Rosen Publishing Group, Inc.

All rights reserved. No part of this book may be reproduced in any form without permission in writing from the publisher, except by a reviewer.

First Edition

Editor: Melissa Raé Shofner
Book Design: Reann Nye

Photo Credits: Seriest art Bplanet/Shutterstock.com; cover wavebreakmedia/ Shutterstock.com; p. 5 Nastasic/DigitalVision Vectors/Getty Images; p. 7 Africa Studio/Shutterstock.com; p. 9 Rob Crandall/Shutterstock.com; pp. 11, 21 Hero Images/Getty Images; p. 13 https://commons.wikimedia.org/wiki/File:Russell_ Lee,_Tagged_for_evacuation,_Salinas,_California,_May_1942.jpg; p. 15 Hulton Archive/Getty Images; p. 17 Evan El-Amin/Shutterstock.com; p. 19 Everett Historical/Shutterstock.com; p. 22 wavebreakmedia/Shutterstock.com.

Cataloging-in-Publication Data

Names: Turner, Joshua.
Title: What is majority rule? / Joshua Turner.
Description: New York : PowerKids Press, 2020. | Series: The principles of democracy | Includes glossary and index.
Identifiers: ISBN 9781538342800 (pbk.) | ISBN 9781538342824 (library bound) | ISBN 9781538342817 (6 pack)
Subjects: LCSH: Proportional representation–United States–Juvenile literature. | Majorities–Juvenile literature. | Minorities–Civil rights–United States–Juvenile literature. | Democracy–United States–Juvenile literature.
Classification: LCC JF1075.U6 T87 2019 | DDC 323.5–dc23

Manufactured in the United States of America

CPSIA Compliance Information: Batch #CSPK19: For Further Information contact Rosen Publishing, New York, New York at 1-800-237-9932

CONTENTS

★ ★ ★ ★ ★ ★ ★ ★ ★ ★

WHAT IS MAJORITY RULE? 4

FAIRNESS AND COMPROMISE 6

MAJORITY RULE
    AND DEMOCRACY 10

WHEN IS MAJORITY RULE BAD? . . . 12

PROTECTION OF THE MINORITY . . . 14

IS THE MAJORITY
    ALWAYS RIGHT? 16

MAJORITY VS. MINORITY RULE . . . 18

THE IMPORTANCE OF
    CIVIC DUTY 20

ALWAYS BE HEARD 22

GLOSSARY 23

INDEX 24

WEBSITES 24

WHAT IS MAJORITY RULE?

The United States is a republic, which is a form of democratic government in which people vote for representatives to make decisions. Representatives are people who represent, or speak for, citizens in government.

One of the most important parts of a democracy is the idea of majority rule. If more people support and vote for a **candidate**, that candidate wins the election. If more people support a law or a **policy**, that policy or law is **enacted**.

THE SPIRIT OF DEMOCRACY

Ancient Rome was one of the first republics. Citizens voted for senators to represent them and their interests. The Founding Fathers of the United States tried to copy Rome when setting up the country's new government.

Majority rule and democracy date back more than 2,000 years, all the way to ancient Greece and Rome.

5

FAIRNESS AND COMPROMISE

★ ★ ★ ★ ★ ★ ★ ★ ★ ★ ★

One reason majority rule is appealing is because it seems fair. For example, a group of five friends wants to order a pizza. If only two friends want vegetables as toppings, it's not fair to have only vegetables on the whole pizza.

Since more people don't want vegetables, the majority rules. The majority may decide to put no vegetables on the pizza. Or they may compromise and put vegetables on half to make the minority happy.

When people compromise, it means they reach an agreement in which each side gives up something they want in order to avoid or end an argument.

★ ★ ★ ★ ★ ★ ★ ★ ★

Compromise is necessary in a democracy, even when you're in the majority. When laws get made, they need the support of many representatives. They must pass in the House of Representatives and the Senate. Finally, they must be signed into law by the president.

For a law to gain majority support, lawmakers must compromise on certain positions to make a greater number of people happy. This means even the majority might not get everything it wants. The final law, however, will appeal to more people.

> In a democracy, the majority gets to decide what the laws are and who will be in the government.

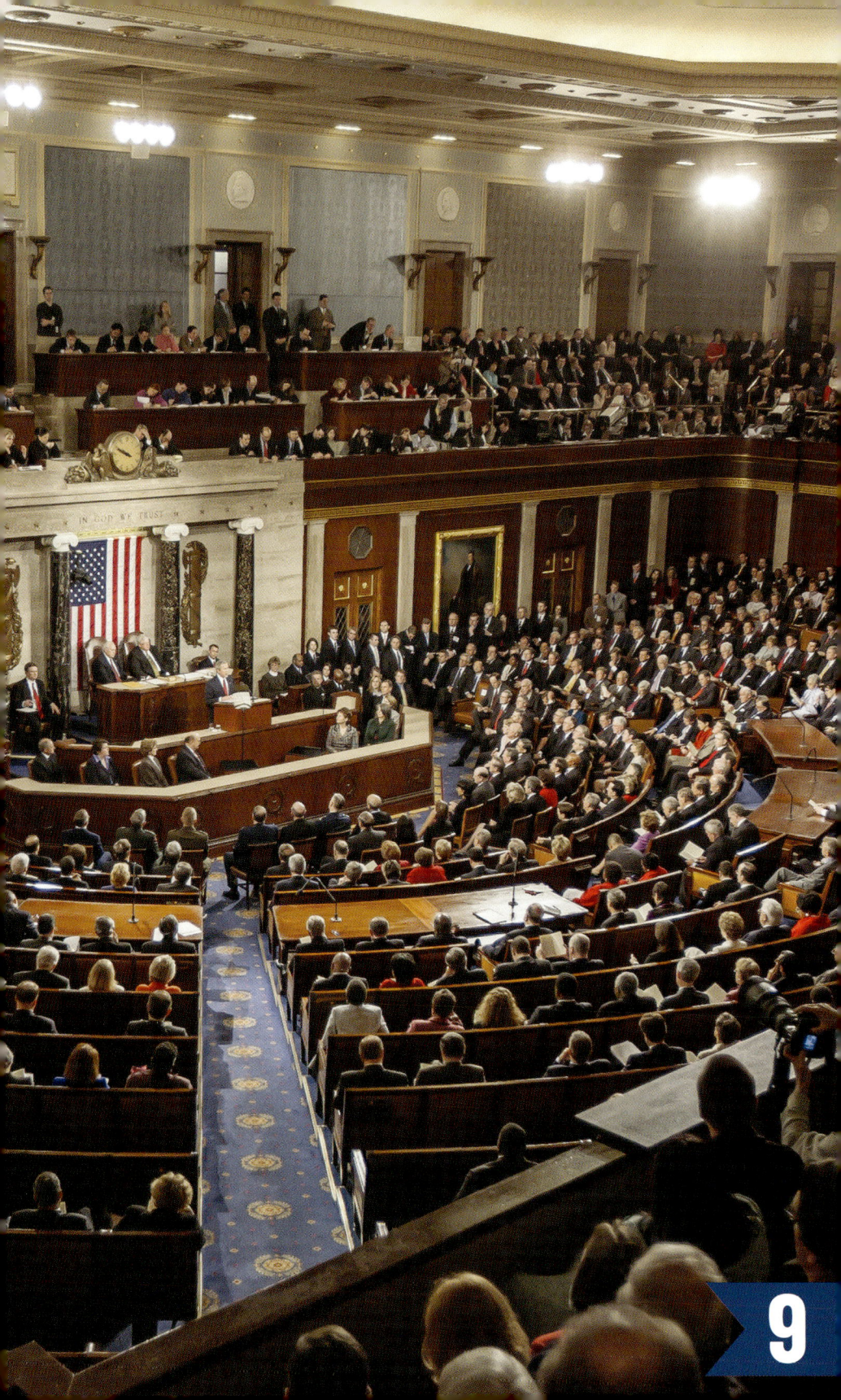

MAJORITY RULE AND DEMOCRACY

In a democracy, the majority make its voice heard through elections. Representatives are chosen by a majority vote. These elected officials then pass laws. They hope the majority agrees with their decisions. If they do a good job, the majority will reelect them when their term is up.

There are other ways for the majority to be heard in a democracy, too. In a referendum, lawmakers don't vote on the issues. Instead, the population gets to decide directly. They vote to choose if a policy should become law.

THE SPIRIT OF DEMOCRACY

The first election in the United States was held in 1788. In this election, George Washington won the first of his two terms as president. Washington won **unanimously.**

Voting, whether for a candidate or for an issue, is how the majority's voice is heard in a democracy.

WHEN IS MAJORITY RULE BAD?

★ ★ ★ ★ ★ ★ ★ ★ ★ ★

When majority rule goes bad, it's called the **tyranny** of the majority. When this happens, **minority** groups are mistreated because their views are different from those of the majority. A majority candidate may enact laws that are good for the majority without thinking about the rights or wellbeing of the minority.

In the United States, this happened right after the Civil War, when Southern states voted to **segregate** blacks from whites. It happened again during World War II when Japanese Americans were placed in **internment** camps.

Majority rule can sometimes lead to bad decisions, such as the decision to place Japanese Americans in camps during World War II.

13

PROTECTION OF THE MINORITY

Majority rule can sometimes lead to minority groups being harmed. This means the **protection** of minority rights is very important in a democracy. In the United States, minority rights are protected through **activism** and amendments, or changes, to the Constitution.

Activist movements help protect minorities. Historic movements have protected rights for voters, women, workers, and people of color. The majority still rules, but it is stopped from continuing unfair and dangerous majority policies.

THE SPIRIT OF DEMOCRACY

Martin Luther King Jr. was one of the most important civil rights activists in U.S. history. He spent his life protecting minorities and fighting for the rights of African Americans, workers, and poor citizens.

Protection of the minority happens when activists bring attention to bad laws or harmful actions of the majority.

IS THE MAJORITY ALWAYS RIGHT?

★ ★ ★ ★ ★ ★ ★ ★ ★ ★

If a majority of people believe something, often that means it's morally or factually correct. However, majority rule sometimes gets it wrong. The majority might support a war that turns out badly. Or the majority could support a candidate who isn't a good leader.

The United States has minority protections because we know the majority can get it wrong. A person should never feel bad or wrong for being in the minority.

★ ★ ★ ★ ★ ★ ★ ★ ★ ★

THE SPIRIT OF DEMOCRACY

Alexander Hamilton, one of the Founding Fathers, helped shape the Constitution and the United States government. He made sure it wouldn't be too easy for the majority to always get its way.

★ ★ ★ ★ ★ ★ ★ ★ ★

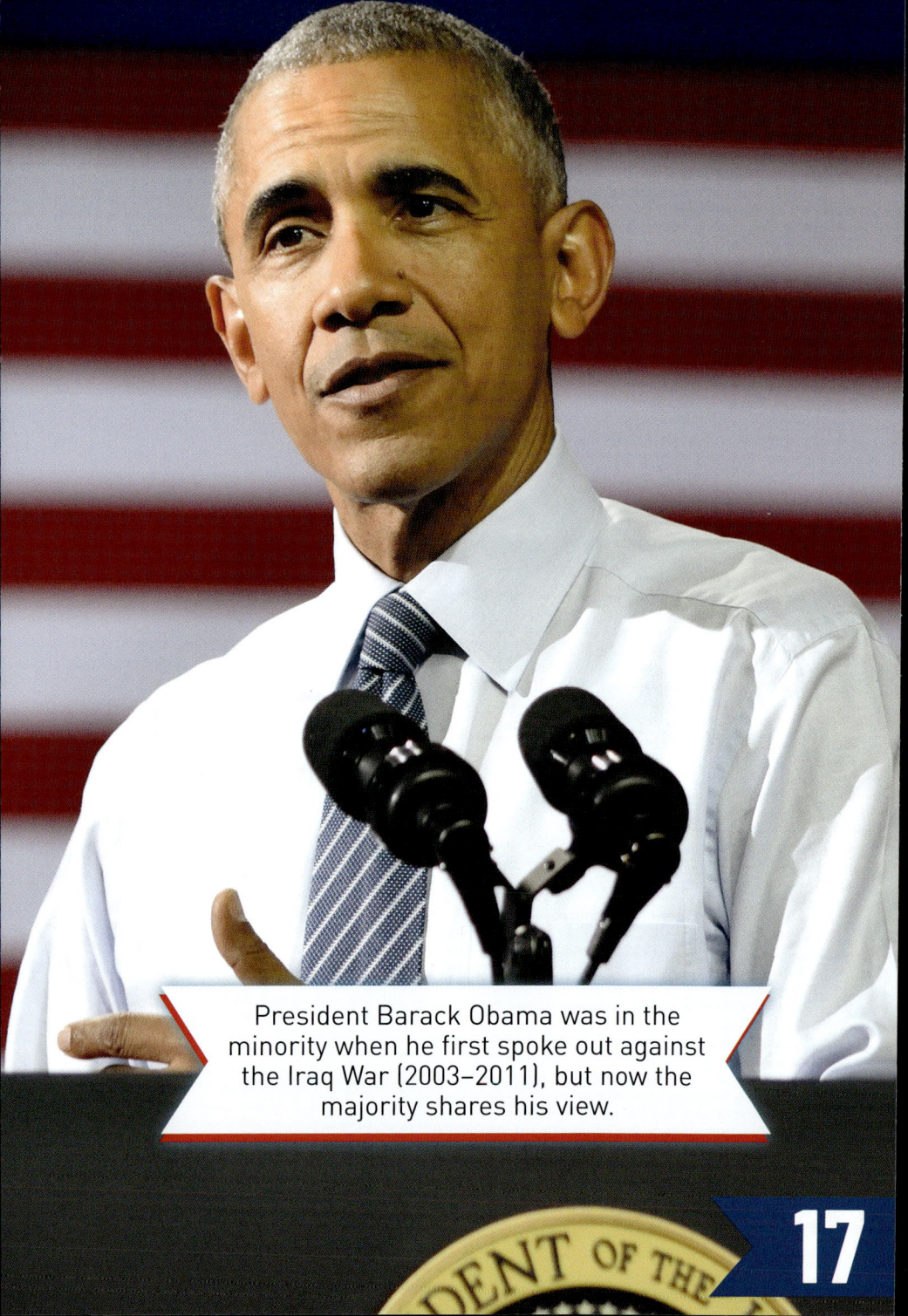

President Barack Obama was in the minority when he first spoke out against the Iraq War (2003–2011), but now the majority shares his view.

MAJORITY VS. MINORITY RULE

What separates democracy from other kinds of government? In a democracy, the minority doesn't rule, but in nondemocratic countries the minority can rule over the majority.

This often has bad results for the country's citizens if their majority views don't match up with the leading minority. It can lead to **repression** and dangerous conditions for the majority of people. One of the reasons the United States became a country was because people wanted out from under the minority rule of the king of England.

In the late 1700s, George Washington led the United States in the Revolutionary War to end the minority rule of the king of England.

19

THE IMPORTANCE OF CIVIC DUTY

In order for the majority to rule well, every citizen must do their civic duty. This means citizens need to vote in elections and pay attention to the news. They must also understand the issues facing their country.

A good majority is an **informed** majority. A good majority also understands what the minority view is, even if they don't agree with it. For majority rule to be fair and benefit as many people as possible, every person must play his or her part.

THE SPIRIT OF DEMOCRACY

Thomas Jefferson, our nation's third president, was a big supporter of public education. He believed it was the only way for the majority of citizens to be informed and make good decisions about government.

A good way for citizens to perform their civic duty is to attend town hall meetings with their representatives.

ALWAYS BE HEARD

In your life, you'll have views and opinions that will sometimes be in the majority and sometimes be in the minority. In a democracy, one of the most important acts you can do as a citizen is make your voice heard.

If you're in the majority, this adds another important voice. If you're in the minority, this adds an important **dissent** that may convince other people. Either way, people need to speak out, so society can know where the majority lies.

GLOSSARY

activism: Acting strongly in support of or against an issue.

candidate: Someone who is being considered for a job, position, or award.

dissent: A public disagreement with an official opinion, decision, or set of beliefs.

enact: To make something officially part of the law.

informed: Having information or knowledge about something.

internment: The act of putting someone in a prison for political reasons during a war.

minority: The group that is the smaller part of a larger group.

policy: An officially accepted set of rules or ideas about what should be done.

protection: The act of keeping something safe from harm.

repression: The act of using force to control someone or something.

segregate: To separate people based on race, class, or ethnicity.

tyranny: Cruel and unfair treatment by people with power over others.

unanimous: Agreed to by everyone.

INDEX

A
activism, 14

C
candidates, 4, 12
compromise, 6, 8

D
dissent, 22

E
elections, 10, 20

H
House of Representatives, 8

L
laws, 4, 8, 10

M
minorities, 12, 14, 16, 18, 22

P
president, 8

R
referendum, 10
repression, 18

S
Senate, 8

T
tyranny of the majority, 12

WEBSITES

Due to the changing nature of Internet links, PowerKids Press has developed an online list of websites related to the subject of this book. This site is updated regularly. Please use this link to access the list: www.powerkidslinks.com/pofd/maj